OPERA BUFFA

TOMAŽ ŠALAMUN

Opera Buffa

Tomaž Šalamun

Translated by Matthew Moore

Black Ocean
Boston - Chicago

Black Ocean
P.O. Box 52030
Boston, MA 02205
blackocean.org

ISBN: 978-1-939568-42-7

Library of Congress Control Number: 2021946802

FIRST EDITION

Translator's Preface

Tomaž Šalamun's *Opera Buffa* was first published in Slovenia by Goga Publishing House in February 2011. Tomaž Šalamun and I met the same year, in Austin, Texas, where he was a visiting instructor and I was a graduate fellow at the Michener Center for Writers. At his suggestion, he and I began work on translations that went on just a few years, most of it via email, and, in a treasured part of a summer in 2012, together in Ljubljana. In Austin, we dined at Vespaio, ate seafood pasta and drank barolo and calva, talked about Herman Melville, and the primordial humors of poesis. In Ljubljana, we worked most days upstairs at Čajna hiša Cha and one afternoon in an enormous hotel cafeteria. Some time passed, some poems translated, others to be accomplished, but the translation flood he and I coasted on in 2011 and 2012 was not gained again.

In 2014, Tomaž Šalamun died in Ljubljana—in the week between Christmas Day and New Year's Day; in that week that brims with evanescence; on the day in 1938 the great poet Osip Mandelstam died imprisoned in Vladivostok; on the day in 537 the Hagia Sofia was completed—on December 27. In the wake of his loss, heavy grief rolled an immobilizing, sheet-rock vacant lot over the mellifluous facets of Šalamun's poems after Šalamun. So what was I to do with the unfinished translations, could I do them alone, and, oh hell, did I have whatever at all a right to do so, without their bird-eyed, soft-spoken, courtly, Slovenian chevalier?

When he and I translated the *Opera Buffa* poems, under the groin-vaulted ceilings in the tea-house on Ljubljana's old town square, a holdout for poets in their youth and the aging prime, Tomaž said: there is no intelligence in these poems, they go how they go. He slapped the table like of course, like no exit from the poem. The cast iron teapot dampened edges of sheaves, porcelain tea plates ringed poems like whistling halos. Tomaž read his Slovar. No, he said, that line isn't meaning anything, it is totally moronic, not looking up, it is what a moron says, looking bright ahead. Tomaž would diagram the *Opera Buffa* poems with a stylite's attention, marooned in the nonsense of the commons that shapes the slapstick of milling voices above and below, where epochs, mythologies, and populations run together in the gathers. He called the *Opera Buffa* poems his lollygagging, idiotic children, and he meant it as sweet as a shepherd speaks for his flock, with the clarity of a vision visit in which an anchoress looks on a shaft of light that speaks to god. These wide-eyed poems lay in the hay with the animals, foundered in clouds above the sea, lapping seawalls between the negative ecologies of populations. The poems stretched their legs and stood in the shadow of awe's negation.

Some of the *Opera Buffa* poems were cotranslated in the vernacular of epithet. Tomaž and I would sound our voices down the page, in the hammered, flattened effect of an anchor that plummets, and take the measure of each line for hitches, loops, tangles, and errancies, till the lines ran down the page in a united motion. The poem, when finished, would become one syllabic plosive, an animal architecture of imagination unfurling across a profane scroll of histories and beliefs, games and refusals. Tomaž had a lot of physically precise gestures at the ready to helm these living vessels. His hands would conduct the lines down the pages. Tomaž asked for the American grain of a phrase, I'd give it, and we took turns dropping the phrase on its head. The parts of speech fell perforce, fell out per Celan's Hamlet: a king is a thing . . . a shell is a sex is a sea . . . nothing is a metaphor . . . what each poem-hold holds in common is a nacre. Tomaž's words left our bodies, the poem became their body, and it jumped into water, over and over, a dumb child throwing and fetching her branch using only her teeth.

For the poem "Barkovlje," Tomaž wanted the first line of the fifth stanza to end with saliva caught by a boom microphone in a production of a film, specifically Werner Herzog's. We began with no phrase for a placeholder, a usual enough occurrence, but that meant we had no target. Tomaž said, "Choory Moory's wife//swallowed saliva. It boomed." He said again, "it boomed.:" I said it, "it boomed." Tomaž went through words that catch sound, snapping his fingers: "it banged, it called, it picked up, it echoed." "It exploded," I said, fixed on the earlier lines, "In the planes//we circled above Bistrica." "No," Tomaž said, "the line has no," and he hit the table calmly to prove what he didn't want. The impact, the event. He snapped his fingers. We went through a dozen sounds. None held what Tomaž held in his mind. Eventually, I said, "what is there in the line," and Tomaž said, "sound that is going and caught, together." He looked impatient. Tomaž was fast. With doubt Tomaž would accept, I said, "it soundeded." Tomaž said, "what, no, what is, 'soundeded,' that's nothing, you mean sounded." We had done "sounded," it was dismissed immediately, with a certain furor. I said, "you pick up what sounded, it sounded-ed." Tomaž said, "I don't think 'it soundeded,' only 'soundeded.' 'Choory Moory's wife swallowed saliva. Soundeded.'" He read the whole poem, snapping his fingers at "Soundeded." He would go, I was caught, our rehearsals of language ran parallel to his orchestration of gestures, seeking the poems he went after and got.

Time passed badly after Tomaž died. Then, Janaka Stucky's Black Ocean began to publish an elegant posthumous book series of Šalamun's translated work in 2015. Reading Šalamun's work vitalized by Black Ocean, in turn, vitalized my efforts to make happen what Šalamun would have wanted. Close friends encouraged me to reach out to Black Ocean, and possibilities began to grow roots. *Andes* (2016) and *Druids* (2019) were published next, in Black Ocean's singular effort to vitalize and honor Šalamun's life work as the formidable contribution to 20th and 21st-century Central European poetries that it is. Black Ocean was patient and kind. In this time, I got sober, in 2016, and, in 2020, began to learn to live in recovery. With a digital copy of the 2011 Goga publication, I began to translate *Opera Buffa* using online Slovars and multiple translation engines and dictionaries. I installed a system of tactics. I would translate a poem from Slovenian to English, then English to Slovenian, and then run both of the translated versions of the poems through a separate set of dictionaries and engines, whittling down mistakes. I began many cigarettes and conversations in my head with memories of Šalamun. I began to recall conversations on poems that he and I had had in Ljubljana, in which referents had escaped us both, and sought out the particulars. I began research into the Slovenian, Mediterranean, and global historical polysemy that the *Opera Buffa* poems hold, in the proper nouns which are wound, with immanence and violence, around the forms of their blasted sonnets and fragments.

So what, OK, what is opera buffa? Opera buffa was a genre of the late 18th-century Italian comedic opera, rooted in Naples, celebrated by Turin's early capital, performed all over Nord Italia. Opera buffa rose to popularity in the epoch between Risorgimento and irredentism, as the desire for state unification reached militant nationalism. Its production faded near 1893, when Giuseppe Verdi, the favorite composer of the hard-line nationalists, staged *Falstaff* in Milan, just as proto-Fascism would begin to dawn. Opera buffa was a light genre, romantic and slapstick, regional and low-brow, performed in local dialects, about local characters or figures, on the local streets, embroiled in locally relevant ordeals. Opera buffa's heroes and villains were sweethearts and struggling workers, the love rivals and moronic bosses, greedy landlords, chaotic families, and gossiping neighbors. As a genre, opera buffa began as intermezzo, broad fare to segment the epic durations and the tragic dimensions of opera's prestige genre, opera seria.

Opera buffa would replenish audiences' emotional stamina; its high-caloric pleasures—the bawdy antics, the merry melodies, and the duck soup buffoons—would give the house some food to sustain opera seria's next sublime act of noble morals and grievous consequence.

So what, OK, what is a poetry translation into written English? Poetry translation into written English needs the translator to provide the discrete language that goes against written English, literal translation, and correct word choice; the discrete language that deems unpoetic what a poem's reader would presume written English needs. Silly written English dependencies on propriety and property, such as grammar that always agrees, sentences that are always complete, and total structural integrity; all of which has nothing to do with poetry. Poetry translation into written English must reside in the poem-heart, and in poem-time, to provide the indifference of poetry with discrete language to get a poem through the difference in languages alive. Written English is rarely discrete, unless it omits, or condenses. Written English likes to explain, with words. Why, saying it, I notice, why, wouldn't now be the time to do away with the unpoetic habits in written English? Why, yes: now's the time! Poetry translation into written English only needs a translator to accept the moods of histories and the genealogies of allusions behind poetry. I don't know Slovenian. I don't think you need to train in languages to translate a poem very well. Just accept a poem's discrete language, keep several dictionaries and grammar books open on the desk as you work; after that, you just have to accept all of the coming critiques.

So what, OK, what is Tomaž Šalamun's *Opera Buffa*? It is the poetry of an afterlife of histories fallen on earth's surface, whose lines form melancholy and jubilant rings of gravity and grace, some kind of value-neutral heaven pooling between the slats on the floors of atrocities from hell. Forced Italianization of indigenous Slavic peoples; Vatican-Ustaše genocide against subaltern populations across the Nazi puppet state of the ISC; the concentration camps in Gonars, Padova, Renicci, and Rab; post-war Partisan reprisals against the collaborationists and bystanders to Fascist mass killings; the contemporary liberal democracies' wars, vicious prejudices, and internment policies against racialized populations forced to migrate from MENA and India due to external and internal campaigns of oppression and subjection. Hell on earth would be better served by opera seria, so what would opera buffa be, in the middle of the acts of total human horror, what would begin to feel heavenly? Nothing good, really, comic only insofar as mirrors snort before perpetrators who imagine they are innocents—is it humorous to imagine that inno-cence could exist here? Local in a sense that descendants of massacred village O would identify as survivors even if their ancestors had massacred village B. If you cut a slice of the historicized bloodletting, the eastern Mediterranean earth would appear marbled with populations burying each other under each other, over and over, in the most grimacing intersectional fashion. Tomaž Šalamun's poetic vision of opera buffa holds that meaning is a terrible dependence: on who is speaking and who is listening, or who remains silent; on the fact that one neighbor's comforters are, will be, or have been, another neighbor's violators; on history's promise that what is human is not any kind of enlightenment. Only poetry, non-human, and absolute collective memory can voice all realistic facts of immanence, the senseless and impenetrable realities which people deny, take for granted, and reject outright.

Populations of breath, words, substantiate the poem as geological, material, historical event on earth. The poem is a study of the profanations that grow primordial roots in language, roots to lead one to encounter the geodes of rime, patterns in the petals in etymological networks, and slime that trails from the protein-chain of histories on the underside of words. The poem is spell-work not by dint of words, yet by things words bear in their names, the surfaces on which aural activity transubstantiates objects, and the depths through which time's glottal erosions and accumulations produce the contexture of things words stand for, as earthen blazons. Reism, the passion study that believes the phrase *a flower* is a flower, says that to kidnap a word into the symbolic order, away from architectonics, away from the ardor of the thing itself, is one step toward Fascist, nationalist violences (1), violences in which a word is only significant in its properties, to whom and what it belongs, and in which a word is never to be held close as it's being on the verge of the thing itself, in the populations of breath. "Snow," is an object lesson in reism, in the substantiation of words on the absolute verge of the event of the things itself, no distance between lightning and thunder, no mimetic layer between what "it's" that lights the fire of the tongue to and what "it is," that appears to be, and appears to be again, albeit with the differ-ence of repetition, the ambient lambency and gravity of poetry that Šalamun anchors to the weight and light of snow, the spirit of the mechanics of lines in depth. In 1960, a poet from Czernowitz, whose anagrammatic pen-name echoes the word porcelain, gave a speech for a prize, in which among his first remarks to his audience, ladies and gentlemen, stands a remark about a conversation, which occurs in a play about revolution, slaughter, populations, and sacrifice, about the exercise of breath, the experiment of breath as passage, between two figures, conver-sation the poet says would go on forever without snags. "There are," he says to his audience, ladies and gentlemen, in the passage-work between the populations of breath, "snags" (2). Šal-amun's poem "Minerals," presents the excavation of the populations of breath as geological, time-burdened snags, and oriented beyond roots in human witness amid the limit-points of life and death; instead, the poem is all flungness, spun-ness, a value-neutral sublimation of all rec-orded matter into seraphic process.

Except for three Simonidean fragments, each *Opera Buffa* poem is a kind of mold spore born on the Clare sonnet; each poem is seven couplets, each one full of affinities and divisions, replete with pivots and feet; each line has a power of a little volta ghost in it. Near uniform arrangement and formal repetition in couplet sonnets shape a blazing alterity of contexture and syntax in individual lines to give the *Opera Buffa* poems their flowering, rotting stature as oxymoronic sonnets. These poems oppose their readers as much as they oppose themselves; their tone feigns as often as it gnashes; they are bound to flowing aberration and riddled with choiceless choice. The *Opera Buffa* poems hold such fixed patterns that their constancy veers between proliferation and destruction; the couplet sonnets pull lines apart that wire together meaning, the lines broken into ranks that want to break rank again. Or, these are not ranks at all, instead, the couplets are: tracks on railroads; bars on prison cells; detachments on patrol; nails. Nails? Nails, yes, hobbed from their wire. The *Opera Buffa* poems enact lines from an early Šalamun poem, "Eclipse II," that the author Christopher Merrill set to title his own literary travelogue of Central Europe in the 1990's, *Only the Nails Remain: Scenes from the Balkan Wars*: "Only the nails will remain, | all welded together and rusty. | So I will remain. | So I will survive everything." (3). The *Opera Buffa* poems are the nails that survive everything, sharp with memories and histories, blunt with places and names, sharpened by time's erosion, blunted by external forces. My job as a translator was to make the poems hit how they hit and ring in written English the way they hit and ring in Šalamun's languages. These translations are just a little jet of rust in the Šalamunian night.

Matthew Moore
New Orleans, Fall 2021

Postscript

About the *Opera Buffa* poems, Tomaž said they were doubtless the most possessed and insane he had written, full of agon, memoria, nonsense. He refused to make sense of their proclivities and habits, had no map including their origin. The *Opera Buffa* poems are the after-life of a political poetry. None of them have a due purpose, but they do owe, and they are owed.

1. Ales Debeljak, "Tomaž Šalamun and His "Tribe"." Agni, no. 59 (2004): 167-175. Accessed July 1, 2021. http://www.jstor. org/stable/23010839.

2. Paul Celan, trans. Rosemarie Waldrop, Collected Prose (New York: Routledge, 2003), 37.

3. Merrill, Christopher. Only the Nails Remain: Scenes from the Balkan Wars. Rowman & Littlefield: Lanham, MD. 2001. p. 42.

CONTENTS

agents of Leviathan
can be bought
they have no sense of fate
they are the functionaries of chance

—Zbigniew Herbert, "Jonah"

SNOW

Rouge. It's not a rose, it's rouge.
It's a smile. It's a seal.

They are eyes. It's the forehead.
It's the kouros. Naxos.

They are hair. It is a gas village.
It's winter. It's spring.

It's an arm broken off.
It's vomiting.

It's hot.
It's not a ticket.

It's waiting.
It's a ticket. Map.

It's Europe.
Zeus abducts the Americas.

"NOW THERE IS NO ONE LEFT. THAT'S A GOOD CONTINUATION"

Beckett, Ashkenazi have in
footsoles grass,

Chinese junks, nightgowns
drawstring. Five steps

is five steps. This is not
no coronation.

For drama or a sandbag.
For

drama! For drama! For
floral Cyrillic

struggle! In space we
stumble

at the fork. In silence the
club laughs.

WHEN THE OWL WASHES THE CANVAS

To open the faucets, Anastasia,
will bring you to naught

nowhere. We watched the heat.
A figure is a face, a part,

motif. Sulfur on a barrel. A distance
roosters advertise. A gull

screams. The child sleeps. A willow
leaf decides to sail. The man

parts his golden hair behind
the bay head, and strolls

outside the hotel. I dreamed
what Andraž read,

out loud. Then he slumped between
pillows. The dream is gone.

WHITE AUBERGINE THOROUGHBREDS
CHURN UP THE SOIL

Horses, from the infamous to
the venerable, fall

a tree to its base and crush its
roots. They sweat,

exasperate. Spring is in the
invisible hairs of their hide.

The count cannot count
the verticals. In summer,

centipedes eat vegetation
by tons, as the bit and the

saddle blush blood. Why not
use his boat? Does he not

have one? He does! He does!
Like the lure in him that cuts.

OSMOSIS IS CLINICAL

Defenders of rocks, children of deserts,
the geraniums burn.

Images circulate from
underground. Heart

of quinine, open the shy
wound. They pose.

I pose. He himself
poses. We piss on

the plaque from the library roof.
Will you savor this,

flare your nostrils? Alexandrian
chime, iron hooves,

horses. Remember, how it burned?
How your hand went to your chin?

STJEPAN RADIĆ STREET

Obedient lion, who do you believe? Who do
you lean your coin on? Bluecap

is gonna cut your head off. The scalps round
up, shave and suffer. The hearts

go to ground. Magnificent. No Adriatic wind
to touch Velebit, no bakeries to

bask. Nothing is wrong with you. Time runs
head-on. Under arches, the red

shirt vanishes, a squirrel with a tail. With an
ornament. Snows as lumpen as

corpses are consequences of car
accidents. Microwave

ovens acclimate the changes of
the history of the flesh.

FROM THE KEY TO THE WHITE BONE

Protean mark library with the rusted
aeration, sit on that stone.

Sleep, lift your tits. Spiel sedge, it is
time, good morning, Dule; who will

whet our religious sword, who it
will wash. The bells cast the toll.

Now they don't.
The bird I see laterally is gray,

a dove, probably, she disappeared too.
The bush is a very nasal lady.

The elephant master is a child of bliss.
The loess boils us. Sleep light,

hunger. Sleep light, hunger. Wash with
a cloth. Please don't get your hair wet.

THE DIFFERENCE FROM ENTRANCE TO EXIT AT THE FRANCIS BACON RETROSPECTIVE AT MUSEO CORRER

O, white chapter's abrasions!
Spar-hawk, gash yourself!

I'm wrapped in your stole.
The era flashed me into

kara luck in the sea common.
You row a sky, you row a

kid. Fir cones whirl in the tiger's
mouth. Little orbs crunch.

Ho! How your sweater gleams!
You put it on. You take it

off. How do I boil it? A mottled
parrot? The real data hit

my head like a true ink. I hardly
stammered out: BTC.

TO NAME WHITE GOATS WHAT THEY BITE

You are a congealed plane tree.
Shelley and wine and blood.

It's a cross. It's chains. It's a wet
white egg. It's a steamboat,

it comes in and goes out at night.
In the port, far from the

Alps. Water foams, water spins a
leaf. The lobbies light

the channel. I open a parasol.
Penetrate a village. Wind

blows northeast, though the
annunciation disagrees. My

hand is dry, and formula A enters
the body of the colossus.

IVES, I DID NOT LOOK AT THE FINISH LINE

You change horizons, too, when
you swallow saliva, dear

reader. We play with image like
the indigenous, Italicized.

I take whatever I'm prescribed,
low behavior's

low behaviors. I did enjoy the
ortolans (I don't

eat them, like Italians, no, no,
I enjoyed them

as they sang). I pushed the ship
away. I just asked for a little bit.

Hi, c'mon, hi, clutching something
makes it more expensive.

PITAGORA'S REDCAPS

The clones are made of Carrara
marble. They have hard

times to survive. How the tufts
grow in houses. In vain.

With the scum in 'em that
rhymes. My bed entwines

buildings. They deliver the bread.
They jump out of the van.

They listen to the radio. Engines
rustle and the doors thud

shut. Please, would you give me,
from the green one, cigarette burek.

From five boys, a giant, basketed
stalk is produced to grow.

TO LUNCH THE SACKCLOTH

Stay in position. Stay in touch.
Collect and wash. Lord

Kinch, the blade. Chains sniff,
snuff. Prisoner, step off

the transfer bus. Sally port!
What you hold

is dark in the mouth! Is it
sewn, from the mill?

Is it ashen, from hot
apples?

Bang! To think how a spider sees
pulls like pliers.

It's lightning. Collate the chrome
against the dross.

ALL WILL COME, THE TITS ON THE STROLLER

If entelechy is the enchilada, it is me,
Gavroche.

Picasso was made from fodder cream
of masses.

You are Black.
You are from Kerala.

How you rowed
said you earned more

here. Time jumps out
and you will

hatch, the advice of the tailors'
subjects. *These are*

thugs. They stole everything from
the people.

TO STAND ON TIPTOES

Frugal rival. To stand on tiptoes with heavenly
Aida. Oh, lotion, slick

expert, fluted in the sarcophagus
and the inspection tent.

Oh, lotion, flies incline on daubs
from acqua modificata.

Elephants are achromatic. The porters are sore.
Rose land wreathes you.

I see a faery fly into a sand dune.
That wind can sure play

the grasses. Orality? Who can coin the scythe?
Who can hear that saw?

I shall wait for the lady,
to punch in after her dinner hour.

THE CROWN ON THE STAND

Fumes are heterogenous, shepherds in
white. Face paint rallies,

to the banners of the serfs, and a mole
is the first cane that rails.

The branch, it segregates,
and it talks.

The crime fertilizes. Ants take a shape
over the left.

There are hands, inside. Concordance rises.
There are no foodstuffs. There's no branch.

It is a forest. Sir Mollusk,
do you know him?

Do you feel the footsteps?
Do you feel the approach?

"CLOUDS HAVE SEQUENCE, BUT NO CONTEXT THAT WE CAN BELIEVE."

Norman Dubie, snatch out the
cougar's eye and use it

to erase. I ruined my battered
dinghy. Burdens

lifted my chin. I licked a clone
to death. Flooded

all my flowers. Mounds lived
in front of him in

houses. We martyred buffalos.
They ran off the

walls. We flashed, pink syringes.
Then came James

Dean. He was small and hideous.
He was big and beautiful.

THE LAKE

Indeed. I returned again, along the
inner edge of Albania to that

wooden hut. Again, there was Bob Hass.
He said: Bogomil Gjuzel is a car

mechanic in Canada. And my reply was:
oh, so for this you gotta have a lot of

guts. The referee inspected me.
I was naked. Like a newborn,

wrapped in a canvas triangle. She
lifted me, smelled me. She was

kind. She lay me down to fight
again. In a nearby shed, rested

men of letters, with sad eyes and
stretched out legs. They all cried.

BARKOVLJE

Dwarfs dried my thigh.
In my eyes, I had

capillaries, boycott, a
groove. In planes, we

circled above Bistrica.
We saw the fires

hounded it. Burnt it like crude
oil. Choory Moory's wife

swallowed saliva. Soundeded.
The one who shot the film on

green ants was there too.
We went to Miramar too.

We brought towels. I recall
the erudite voice.

———

Let's marble the mess of flesh.
Let's put on his briefs.

I raised mine eyes upward.
I saw the closet before me.

Thus powdered the stream, to life and all joy.

IN THE WATER LILY, EXPERIENCED AND JUMPED

Three embroideries bear a heron on
three different poles. The sun scares

undertakers. Whores raise red slabs
on green tables. Thermo-cows,

the mania from the grave, cut it out!
Honey, I asked you

to hand me light today. Did
you press the uniform? Did

you fix up Ottavio's bicycle?
Tinders still lick the

Gothic arch. Grated windows mesh
the lead fed with an

honorific image. Could you so love
a position to take it?

YOU ORGANIZE PEAS AT THE END OF THE NIGHT

Great-grandmother milled a man and
devoured him. She hung over a fence.

He said "Pump!" and disappeared.
Death mixes up coffee and cotton.

Certainly, if he blows, he is bound to be
confused. He has no taste for croissants,

you know. Death is worn out; gasoline
is poured out. She likes to bear crosses

and problems. She stuns Death too. Over
and over, again. Let's applaud her. Death

drags her to a sidewalk, by the throat.
She is pale; she got it wrong. There's

no vineyard. But he's thrown off. And the heart
begins, to tick again, the lithely, little crocodile.

I'M ALREADY SPREADING

The turkey wounded my chin
because he's [insert religion].

I stood right above
him at the podium.

The bison, as only flesh
can, ignited. They

watched each other. Fire
covered Asia Minor and

Cape Horn. The quails
escaped. The youth

started to scream. They
feared to die. Only

my golden children can
varnish their nails.

ALEXANDRA

In the vineyard, we sat, girded by a
cave. Child shoes pinned to

the floor. The shelter began to give,
and walls went dark. You could go

out with a compass, not with wheat.
The ribs carried explosives.

I touched the lady ziptied to me. She
added the extra wheat stalk.

She was Russian. She dripped with
cigarettes. She cheered, on her

husband's grave, what he screamed
in red notebooks. I rowed my

boat and cut my throat. I died mid-
arc. My Adam's apple bobbed.

RICHMOND

Fenjadi was my guru, who I
turned up on the road.

I followed him into the wood.
He followed the woodpecker,

who followed the butterflies,
who followed a woodpecker. We

had our own glass vase each. We
took up the bark the woodpecker

tore down. Inhaled it deeply.
The sun glowed on

the river, and boats were not there.
You, is it yours, the heavenly

soil? Who said this, and to whom,
is not known.

AVE, ITALIANS

Calm the ball. Berta shut her eyes.
Now Berta has no eyes.

Little men will come, wrapped in
sheets, to drown in Maremma.

They'll bring the fog on their little
braids, they'll play with

rackets. They'll have wide eyes,
notches on their foreheads,

and tiny ears like tiny hares.
They'll roll huge barrels

full of volcanoes. The bells
ring. Wholly softly,

I ran across Trieste, the
entirety shot to surface.

TO SOFTEN THE TOUCHMARK WITH A FROTH

With your country complexion, you
flourish

with storms. The tuft is in the axle's
flowers' bed. The bird

upshifts, and around the bend drifts
along its circumferent.

Its corona revolves.
Crests! Remember

the horns of the snails.
The cats mobilized

under the waterfall. They said:
see how it will burn,

it's gonna be awful when
we purr, and they purred.

THE ANCHOR

The swarm does not believe.
The fly believes.

The waiter coerces the ends.
Painter, here is

the showroom! To swallow
thanks to mint.

The cheerful rent boy waves
me over, will I buy him, yes!

Oh, cheerful rent boy, I will,
only I have to save up some,

and wait for my wife to go
to sleep. She's asked me to

put turds in the fridge; wrap
them in tinfoil too, she said.

I WOULD LUNGE INTO THE COTTAGE

Hi, winner, why do you tap me with
a toothpick? Tap, tap,

ditch. Tap, tap, ditch. The invention
is diagnostic and sits

the planet on edge. The paws go into
soil twice. Birds sing.

What, here, can start up a grebe, into
weird, weirder reality?

Engines run and gun. It's all gonna
bud. And roosters roar,

off-the-cuff. Frogs are white, they adore
friction, and bee representatives

are still asleep. They are colorful. White
world, leave, vanish off the earth.

SHE WAS A SECRETARY

When I paused to drink the
orange juice, I woke with

a flat nostril. I rolled a leaf
on tracks (thick as a buoy)

snowbanks and hay stacks
hugged around them.

Where's it look wide open?
Country no. 9, or so?

Agahs had our number. What
we do not know, we

do not know, we said. Agahs
attacked me and died. Agahs

are honorifics to brothers
whose wounds we inflict.

JACKPOT

Insert the tool on the meter.
Bet on that particular karst.

If we hedge against the soft G.
If we hedge on P. He soothes

and he mourns. But even
here, he remains restless,

and he says nothing. He just
thinks it: double it. Silver

can float under it. The chicken
pierces water and drinks

water, and the dragonflies
cannot capture it from the

pond. And he drives a lupin?
Oh, I'd say he drives a lupin.

BILKY WITH A BRIDGE

He jumped. Cut the gas. Spat the coordinates
and followed. His hand broke five bricks, oh hell.

I'm a sentence. I'm a hireling for the bookmaker.
With an optical plastic

carburetor. I race it in
a spattering of cabbage. God is from

Joseph. Praxiteles wears bees. In
Paris, the gloomy footbridge perishes.

Places! Time? Did you rendezvous with the snail?
You are a spindle with quinine.

Ambush. Moses lies on a haystack and
he says, "Bilky with a bridge,"

and repeats the title. Faith is liced and
layered. She keeps her classmate warm.

MINERALS

In the village on the Caspian Sea,
five spun tops

yearn. There's smuggling. There
is ore. I wash

myself out of a hundred
pastes. I study

the crystal and the board.
There are silk

lilies in the crystals. We
use spoons to

mill bread. Black pudding
rose and died.

Nature pulled pure
nothing out of him.

THE SHADOW IN THE TEA

The dwarf gets off the train and swims in a trench.
The rib rings. To obey or not.

The witch ate the salad and counted the stars:
"Mal needs to move her legs."

An aliquot tone is a brigand's delight. I know
Tartars got evicted, their eyes

tube-squeezed out. They settled the shed. Signora
will sell out the piano and not

repent. Enough. Shut up, shut
up, about the boat! The train

moved drowsily. Everybody got torn
up, waiting, pressed to the grey glass.

In the end, the hawthorns and the hawthornesque
beauties. In the end, watch faces escape whetstone.

ITALIANS

They are made as chimneys. If you ice
secretaries, you pick up

small needles. Witches hovered above
the loupe until the loupe

shot through them. Sanskrit's a mortal
action. The thinnest curl.

Bandanas go around the concrete
mixer, you remind me of picarels.

Black glasses are in vogue. Bompiani
celebrated his mussels

and claws. He yawned toward nod.
The people

followed me. Money is for money;
money is not for you.

ANGELINA, ANGELINA, WHAT IS WRONG WITH YOU NOW?

With night come the bees that do not
retreat. Knead your shoulder,

and the bread, held by your shoulder.
The jumper you lubricate can

never forget. Ben-Hur! You are so
willing to gobble hairpins, so

gobble hairpins! To eat grass with
Griboyedov could not mean

forgiveness. The frog is a failure. You
wash with piss but know it right away.

I wish I had the wind. I'd like to have spirits.
I would like wind and spirits.

The rowers gnaw a silver belt.
I see at least two of them here.

THE ANNIVERSARY

Death is a turbot, switched off.
The voice breaks apart. One hundred

and five years of ground lost. The alive
little woodstove sputters.

The Ganges is a dense elder tree. How is it,
that we ladled with a spoon:

lords; ghosts. They fought back like
cooks in the branches. You ran away from

the theater? You did not suffer the death of
your friend? It ignited. Fat

dripped from your father's body.
In Persia, Zoroasters no longer feed

the birds. I called for him.
I never saw him again.

DRULOVKA

The ostrich rocks the boat. He cuts
the ribbon. You unglue from

the roof, span after span. In the
clearing, where we camped.

Where I wanted to spend my youth
with my family. The scull

sank in the grass. What would you
put on a bicycle, if you could

ride a bicycle here? The vault
of your soul? Your menagerie?

Traces of moss? Look through
the human head. She is not the

only one who has a groove. It trickles
out of heaven. You donated your eyes.

THE INSTRUMENT

I'm a statue who sees
distances.

The elephant's muddy
walk pacifies

bootlickers. Cinnamon.
It burns and

reeks. I languored for
days, with a snake.

He basked on river
mud. Include

some heavy metal
trash! Paint it.

In horror, the frogs'
mouths will widen.

TO LUMBERJACK ONE'S OWN SPLENDOUR

The river rolls toward the throat.
The Germans trust their armpits.

I squeezed a wooden fox
to measure, between the

reins, the night. The clocks
always already manifest.

They change her clothes.
They cut her cuticle.

Sometimes it glistens like
a globe. Why don't you

see the grass if it is a globe?
On the globe, everything

would be. I play. Grass
does not lose its clarity.

THE SHELL OF A SHELL

I'm silky, withal a bit infected
ventricle. Wisdom

flowed and ebbed. The naked
lick my forehead.

I stowed my plumage in a cache. So I
wait. I await the jacket. I await

old men to abolish the bloodshed that
pricks the Atsinganoi. Will his

child still grind talents? Along the river
dry meat. That hell-on-hell noise.

The lust for obituaries and red
carnations. Snakes of the Atsinganoi

slither via the corridors. The tree
illumines. The tree sings and illumines.

THE SILENCE COMES

You still fly in the yard without
your head? I doubt it.

The one thing I know is I doubt
the only thing I know

I don't. Beria, so it seems,
strangled him.

He died, it does not seem,
a natural death.

He was my dad. The table was
wiped off with

shavings. The snout loses its
fragrance, and spring and all.

You did not write the addresses
for me to thank you. Best wishes.

THE MARQUIS COMES AND BREAKS THE FIST

Foxes wriggle to grow from me
because I am the earth.

Now they look more like corals.
The water around them

undulates. The strange flower is
a napkin. I see it as I may

watch it from a plane. Sweetest.
Your dark inwardness,

the sunflower, the vase. Silver to
the profligate. Baikal

network, 336 ways in and one
way out. Corals grow from me

since I'm the earth. Plasticines.
All without, water's reservoirs.

BIG MISTAKE

My grandmother drank from a shoe.
But she did not slap Cankar.

Cankar was slapped by Aunt
Mary on the train near

Rakek. You can trust a Russian
to do anything. The cock to die

stilted on excitement. Alright, okay,
aye, with paws? And is Timava

cut to pieces? A man from Vižovlje
at home, who plays the viola?

Why I always remind you.
You and Amir. When Kon-Tiki

took me to Struga, I butchered them,
a descendant of Srečko.

BESTOW ON HIM A WILLOW'S LEAF

Béla, ashtray owner, a wife for
Chomsky and Adam,

Krleža and Chagall had a Bela
too—I courted them

all. The dog frolicks, a fool for
nature. Dazzled there. The clone does not

open the hatch. In the hold, sight is vented
by visions. Clean it, Yoko Ono.

Lose your quarters. Cops upon the brink's
planet transfer quarry.

The totality of the machinery is aroused.
Bright gooseflesh. Trousers have a crease.

This goes to the theater in Trieste
and this goes to the Zurich theater.

THE SYSTEM

A hut with butterflies, a hut with
butterflies. Sand for

two. The miser on embers
screams, but we can't

hear him. We back interest in his
neck, his crust. Binički,

I carried you for water.
The fly got

sick when he bowed his leg. On
yellow oilcloth

the surface can get stuck.
It's like that here,

spacing so as not to be detected
even by M. Kostnapfel.

DAVORIN'S MOMMY TOOK AWAY HIS SCEPTER AND HID IT

The king of surfaces is selfishness.
The cross is stitched into a dimple.

The spume of my elbow.
The soldier of my dream.

What does Davorin say?
How does he watch you?

No pickpocket not already counted
from celluloid and the painted bird.

Genius is tired and dated.
A piece of white wine

erupts from softened nails.
The sun renders two coats

to add to the pile. He shears
the interior and serves dolls.

READ SOVRE'S HOMER

I pissed in mommy's eyes.
It made her worry. I forgot

the key in the smoke. *Addirittura!*
The map is sucking white

thin sheets. Bones at every hour
on different lines. Under a tunic

butter hides, the Heine zone.
More than you braided your hair.

In the Soča Valley behind the hills,
it's hotter than hot! The grebe

of mountains closes her eyes. In one
hand there were flowers stuck

together. Near the river's gentle flow,
dwarves hide. You too? We too.

GOMBO CIRCLED WITH A MATTOCK

Jackals, you craned the spirits
from the rails, therefore

you deserve death. Max Mara,
I merited the little snail,

deplumed the little snail, drew and
quartered the little snail. This

is the last of the fish days. Shut the
manors in the underworld.

The sun marks my newborns with
ribbons. Some of them are

confused. Did you consume spools?
Tuck into parrots. Tuck into parrots.

I flew out of the pit. They
washed me in the black bowl.

FRAGMENTS GIVEN EYES

He who creaks embodies God with his
feet. The rib is a bud.

Veins fill with blood,
hare lips with

cotton. Bacon clothes the horizon
in masks. The sun

gives birth to my children. Yellow
animals are hard and

stingy. Yellow animals
purify the trees.

To kill an elephant, to build
a home. Kocmur! Your

skin is burned! Why! Just go, just
go, take your drama, to the moon!

JACK SPRAT'S POWER WARNS

Masonry's evenings, wall's hatcheries,
I am Tantalus' nephew

and the son of cold capital.
Shepherdess! I stretch

and contract you. The artificial
ear in the mold. Here

on the tables, sense is burning.
Russians flood

the flaw from the outside, and still get
hit by it, moth's chitin.

We restored the heavens to order with
bitter ink from the skies.

The layer is rainbow. The bullfinch is
the signatory on the flag.

PHOTO STORIES, OR FUMETTI

Wayward a boar paddles.
He gains on death.

Pretty powder in a flower head.
In a dream a line recites.

Grandfather grows two bonces
from his bonce. Nine windows.

The sailor walks under flowers
struck with hearts.

Look at it. It is blue, to picture
the sky. Fumetti. Heuristic

strips. Fumetti from the expeller,
descend. Photo stories

and Mali grove. United dwarves.
Each one, hacked off.

YOU CALL AND DIE

You from the white bowels of muddy
marble, make my head

heavy. I governed columns, obelisks,
baths. Marble got tired.

You know, when you don't know, do you know?
Soap lusters are compressed coats of light.

Oh, good morning; oh, is it good? How would we
know, we barely waked.

The perjured one. The dormouse abducted
the pussy and my blouse is orange

and silk. I stepped in the water. I sustained
a stroke. When I got the bone saw

out of me, I pushed the bills that drank
under it and the surface sewed me shut.

HORSE SNORTS IN THE CRYPT

With the story you die instantly. You
call and die. In flanks around

the haven. Washed above the ceiling.
The bee shines. In some parts

it is said boulevards line the hives.
Oh, corpse, you traveled in

the cart with golden wheels. Little
gull on flat feet. Flies, do you

hover above the ears, three-cornered
coals? You covered the eyes of

the charcoal burner with the needles
you pulled from the gigantic

anthills. They were cathedrals. Let's
hope our corpses won't smell.

THEY RUN AROUND WITH STUNTMEN

My newborns run with the sun, already born
with golden lashes and peeled eyes.

Their hair runs amok. Their eyes run to pulp.
The walruses dig up their gold spoor. They are

factory owners. Novices. Jackanapes. When they meet
Beatrice, they surround her body. I see stones

through the water. The light breaks them. It snowed in
Kovačić, who opened his window and mouth.

Pipe organs are black inside. Partisans hoist torches in
them. Then, the snow poured out

into the rain. Rivers rose. Kovačić gave the signal.
They spread their skins on floors and under tables.

And yet, from Kocbek and I, only a drizzle remains.
Gazelles' eyes shine. They don't care about shovels.

BAVA'S NO FUN

I had three sons and five
daughters. They were

chained up in the woods.
Buddha passed them.

He ate a plum. With his
tongue he wet the torn

sail. Where is the plum
pit, greengage?

The police woke up
and set fire to cars.

Their cars were all called
Black Maria. Born

Maria Saltee, a rower. The
mob tended her garden.

IN NEW YORK JAILS

Here's your summons! The owl
stamps it. Stable hands

post at stalls, jockeys at docket.
They hope, a hush tone,

Mr. Groznik might stop along.
And, could you recall

Mr. Groznik? He got busted
in the Bahamas. I ran

the underwear in here
he sent for his brother.

We splashed in great white milk.
From one continent, to the other.

In the tower, Karlica was hot.
In that time, Karlica was drunk.

MILES AND MORE

Fairytale decadents, wrinkled
people. Raise the crazed

animal. Bake her belly. I suck
blue lips in the dust that

melted already. Alexandra's
gunned down, already gone

into debt. I cut my head off slowly,
wipe the sweat of my brow

off the counter. People were kind
to me and savage. Come with me,

come and see, he kissed me, and
he begged me, kindly, oh please,

could he slaughter me? Let me
sunbathe the pillar, dear leader!

HIS LEG WAS REPATRIATED

I found myself in the pirated version,
a gravedigger's hands pushed

into my villi. Sentencehood. Ostrich.
Bulls on his hands. If I step on

the nose of the ship, the ship blows.
If I step on its buttock, the ant shits.

I'm asked why these beasts are
here. I sack them. I toss 'em in

the salted sea. Beasts dyed up to their
necks in crystallography. MacMillan!

Shostakovich and Poulenc frisk each other.
Oxford is blissful. Isaiah folded his covers.

His leg was Ashkali. The waterfall is open
before customary hours. It is hot. It is true.

BATHE MY HAND IN YOURS

Storms pass in Kerala, I fraternize with tigers.
Strange, strange. I died then, too, but

the boat protected me. White ant, black bush.
White bush, black ant. They told me:

wait. In two years, we can settle with
Korea, then we'll dedicate ourselves

to you. If you like it recite it. Luckily,
they did not settle with Korea. Milan

Kučan skipped and whistled with the boss,
and behind him and Havel I totally heeled.

No one touched the bones in my hands
again. Cute boys lined up by sect, CIA

and NKVD, but the report said that my
Metkec chose, to choose the right guru.

WE STRETCHED HIM AND REALIZED HE WAS BULGARIAN

Bishop, the fish is on tiptoes, master,
he is ready to blow the horn. Angles

of lights plank the fence. If the rib is bent,
a circle is made. The stick. We found him

among leaves in the ravine. He had
a stone on his mouth. Marigold rain

fell on little clouds. Probably they hid
him. Probably they dressed him in the

sailing shirt. He did not smoke a
pipe. Braque was not his brother.

He also wore a windbreaker, but
he pushed it in the bush.

We discovered him, on a family
trip, blueberries picked.

LIONS MADE OF BRONZE

Oh stench, oh stench, oh stench, cried
the lady from Slavonska Požega and

cut the elephant with a blade. She's in the
Golden Triangle. Go here to stick pegs in

to measure out the earth. What trout and
beggars dream is what they dream about.

When the dreams come true, they dream
about the King of Kamako. Today, dams

beat all sophistication. Trout climb them.
Strangled glamorous sleep. *Tu peut bien*

faire ta soupe, mais ne mange pas la bétrave.
La bétrave se casse la gueule. Our book

is better than Prešeren. To comb the little
ones. The little ones have peaceable heads.

HABEMUS PAPAM

The niches store the sheds of
snakes. The laugh in the wicker

flask, in the grated white musk.
The majority of Bistritzas.

Shells converge on posters and
in animal bladders. On the

fences twist spoor of sheep.
They scratched themselves.

They were cold. Then they went
to the stall. So, I slid myself

shut with the chain, and leafed
through the monography of

Morandi until the white smoke
announced the new pope.

THE BRUSSELS GARDEN

We seized the family with sponges full,
I mean, we planted them

around the table and tied sponges to the
eyes. They thought they were swallows,

rocked side to side. Some wore sandals.
But Nonno was barefoot.

I read them news then hit them with the
anvil. This is a pharmacy!

Nonno said, disgusted. The table began
rocking. Then stenographers burst in in

balaclavas. After, the storms passed over.
That's how we sacrificed the clan

Ursino. Under them the Chinese women
huddled, their legs hid their faces.

THE BUS STOP

Charles Dickens did beach with peaches,
but there is no reference to this. And

Lady Tudman has a tremendous pension.
Moses grazed on the pasture. I mean,

he was ushered to the desert, to a chilled
glass hut, to wait for the bus:

Abu Dhabi—Dubai. Then sheikh came by, among
horses and falcons. You're shivering, sheik said to

Moses. It's sausage to me. On his left stood a wall
with a peg. The servants were from Kerala.

They stood in boats. You've got a tunic, a train, and
piebald wooden camels, why do you need

a wall? It is so the falcons don't leave us, sheik said.
You're a falcon too, that's why we've come for you.

NOT ME

The vermin attack, and the grasses
grow. God forbid I wear

my trousers washed. I've tarpaulin
on my belly, like

insects. In the teeth of first stories.
Mommy!

Fellini cut, on Cabiria's
throat, and she plunged.

From stumps, we took honey
and rolled it between

our hands. The proto-sesame
pays wildly, but not

me. We sniffed the tiger and
caged it, but not me.

JOŠT WITH A MAJORITY OF BETTORS STARES INTO VELVET

The product of cruel wounds
is the song of white

owls. When they harrow the
run, what will

they say? With Fornazarič in
a paper bag

I rush into the furnace. Nona
shields the washbasin.

Break off the cart
to cash the

hawk. The decision
snaps. Cash

the cart to break off the hawk.
It can't be done.

COUSCOUS AND DARK BLUE

Let's dance, Persian,
you eat great.

Shake your bracelets!

Get moving, Persian,
you eat fine.

Rip off your bracelets!

TITO TOO COULD NOT DRINK THE COMMON SORREL OFFERED TO HIM BY HIS COUSIN IN KUMROVEC

It squeezed my pricky true. I can only drink
Barolo and champagne. Porridge repels me

and bread repels me, it squeezed my pricky
true. The cap, it turned me into a

cur, I turned into a monster. Yesterday, I was
a bell-ringer, a boy with eyes, tender

kernels. They killed me, wrapped me in
a host, buried me. I grow from the grave.

Truly, it squeezed my prick. I can only drink
Barolo and champagne. I die

if there is no brie. The Medici poisoned me
until I became the porn-pope.

They covered me in lollysticks. The children
licked me in the Prater and now this.

———

The age boils. The other age boils,
but won't leave a trace.

The age boils with no sun.
The age boils with sun.